Confirmation

A Congregational Planner

For an in-depth consideration of Lutheran confirmation ministry, see *Confirmation: Engaging Lutheran Foundations and Practices* (Minneapolis: Fortress Press, 1999). This book (ISBN 0-8006-3157-9), available from Augsburg Fortress, Publishers (800-328-4648), offers discussions of the history and theology of confirmation ministry, current models and formats, adolescent development, methodology, content, resources, lifelong education and pastoral ministry, and the role of the congregation as confirming community.

The Confirmation Ministry Task Force Report, adopted by the churchwide assembly of the ELCA in 1993, is a valuable resource for those planning confirmation ministry. This document is foundational for the church and for this planner. The report is available from Augsburg Fortress, Publishers (ISBN 6-0000-2802-4), or as an appendix in the book *Confirmation: Engaging Lutheran Foundations and Practices.*

Confirmation

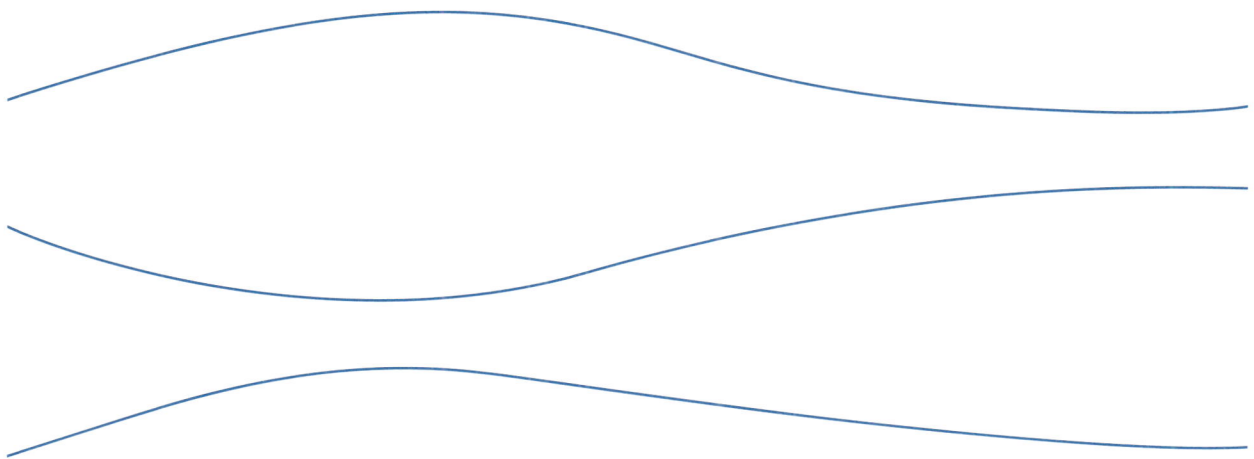

A Congregational Planner

Thomas K. Johnson

Augsburg Fortress, Publishers   Minneapolis

CONTENTS

CONFIRMATION
A Congregational Planner

Editors: Mark Gardner, Eileen K. Zahn, and
Virginia Bonde Zarth
Interior design: Cathy Spengler Design
Interior illustrator: Glenn Quist
Cover design: David Meyer
Cover photo: Chip Porter/TSI

Scripture quotations are from New Revised
Standard Version Bible, copyright © 1989
Division of Christian Education of the
National Council of the Church of Christ in
the United States of America. Used by permission.

Copyright © 1999 Augsburg Fortress
All rights reserved. May not be reproduced.

ISBN 0-8066-3834-6

Manufactured in U.S.A.

1 2 3 4 5 6 7 8 9 0 1 2 3 4 5 6 7 8 9

From the Editors

To the leader: *This planner will help you and a team from your congregation develop and implement a program for confirmation ministry that meets the needs and priorities of your congregation. As you recruit the members of your team, consider all of those in your congregation who have a stake in this ministry: pastor, lay staff, volunteer leaders, parents, youth, and so on. "Confirmation Ministry Team" (pages 43-45), provides a resource for customizing structure, purpose, format, and tasks for the team in your congregation.*

Order a copy of Confirmation: A Congregational Planner *for each team member. Plan on meeting several times over a period of weeks or on a one- or two-day retreat. Invite the participants to complete the Pre-Study Questionnaire (pages 39-40). Then consider each chapter of the planner using the discussion questions provided. Finally, complete the Post-Study Questionnaire (pages 41-43). You will now be ready to design a confirmation ministry program to meet the specific needs and priorities of your congregation.*

INTRODUCTION

HAVE YOU EVER ASKED any of these questions?

- How did the practice of confirmation get started?

- How is confirmation related to baptism?

- Who is doing the confirming and what is being confirmed?

- Was confirmation Martin Luther's idea?

- Why does confirmation mainly focus on adolescents, and is it rite of passage into adulthood?

- How did it become like a graduation ceremony?

- Is confirmation repeatable and can it also be for adults?

Can you answer these questions? As a Lutheran pastor of 12 years, I felt troubled and embarrassed when I realized one day that I could not. I just *did* confirmation the way it was *done to me* and the way the congregation had done it for years. But why? And why did this approach not feel right? Why did it seem more like an academic exercise leading to graduation, than a spiritual experience leading to a lifetime of faith development and discipleship? Something seemed wrong, but I was too busy *doing* confirmation ministry to step back and ask the questions that needed to be asked.

Then I decided to return to school and do some graduate work that would enrich my ministry. To my surprise, and no matter how I tried to ignore them, the confirmation ministry questions kept hounding me. It became clear that I was being led to seek some answers and share what I discovered with others. That's what this planner is about: to prompt you and others in your congregation to ask questions and to seek answers that will help develop a clear vision of what confirmation ministry means and how it should be practiced in your setting. Confirmation, as a ministry of baptismal affirmation, is too important to do blindly or automatically. It is too important to simply expect the pastor to "take care of it." It is time for the whole congregation to take responsibility and get involved. It is time to expand our knowledge about *why* and *how* we do confirmation ministry. This assessment will take some work but will be worthwhile if it helps us better understand and support the work God is doing through confirmation ministry.

The task of shaping the vision for the future of confirmation ministry is a priority across the church. In June 1998 a nation-wide summit was held in Chicago. The symposium, entitled "Confirmation 2000," brought together leaders from different arenas within the church. Participants joined together to ask questions, seek answers, share stories, develop partnerships, and renew the commitment to follow the Holy Spirit's guidance and wisdom. The group recognized and celebrated the creative responses of individual congregations to the challenge of confirmation ministry. The booklet *Confirmation: More Than Just Business as Usual!* (ISBN 6-0000-9992-4) briefly summarizes a variety of approaches to confirmation ministry being used in congregations today. Also, *The Confirmation Ministry Task Force Report*, adopted by the churchwide assembly in September 1993 was reaffirmed as a key resource for direction and discussion. If you do not have a copy of these resources, call Augsburg Fortress at 800-328-4648.

Careful deliberation about confirmation ministry is not a new venture. The 1970 report of the Joint Commission on the Theology and Practice of Confirmation recommended that one's first communion no longer be tied to becoming a confirmed member of the church. The study guide *Confirmation and First Communion: A Study Book* by Frank W. Klos helped the church discuss and understand this recommendation, theologically and historically. It sparked a dramatic shift in the practice of admitting baptized children to the Lord's table. It is a good example of how the power to change comes from communication and the opportunity to engage in dialogue and share what we know and believe to be true.

It is time to renew that dialogue, specifically the recommendation that we understand and practice confirmation, or affirmation of baptism, as a lifelong process rather than a once-in-a-lifetime event. Even though this approach was proposed by the 1970 report, the church was primarily involved in the issue of separating first communion from confirmation. However, the 1993 task force has chosen to reemphasize the invitation to lifelong learning through confirmation ministry:

> Given the lifelong nature of God's act in Baptism and the continuous need for God's Word of grace offered in the shared life and conversations of believers, confirmation ministry is more than education for youth. Issues relating to God's will, faith, and discipleship are important whatever one's age.…While Baptism happens only once, affirmation of Baptism and prayer for the baptized can happen many times.[1]

The task force also recommends the establishment of a confirmation team to help define what confirmation ministry means in the congregation. The team takes responsibility for expanding the ownership of confirmation ministry and relating it to the congregation's total mission. The team is intended to provide support for planning, implementation, and regular evaluation of the congregation's confirmation ministry program with regard to the overriding themes of identity/community, mission/discipleship, and vocation/ministry.

This planner assumes the formation of such a team. Your assignment is to read and discuss the information presented here, develop a vision for an effective confirmation ministry program in your congregation, and then share your findings with the congregation. Please begin by selecting a team leader who will lead you through the job description located in the appendix. Then complete the pre-study questionnaire individually. As you read the guide take time to discuss the questions located at the end of each chapter. Finally, complete the post-study questionnaire. The questionnaires are located at the back of this book.

Confirmation ministry has always focused on "catechesis" or learning through the asking of questions. At baptism the Spirit is given so that we may never stop learning. May the Spirit now guide you to gather the facts and be enlightened, to share opinions and keep an open mind, to test proposals in light of the biblical witness and our theological heritage.

Each time you gather, begin your task by using the following prayer: Dear guiding Spirit, grant us the vision and the strength to reform that which needs to be reformed and the wisdom to sustain that which needs to be sustained. May our response to your grace become a lifetime journey of learning, growing, and serving. May our daily celebration of your baptismal gift grant us the renewed opportunity to affirm all that you are accomplishing through the blessing of confirmation ministry. Strengthen us to serve you as we serve your church. In Christ's name. Amen

Note

1. *Confirmation Ministry Task Force Report* (Evangelical Lutheran Church in America. Adopted by the Churchwide Assembly, September 1, 1993), 9.

CHAPTER I

Confirmation Rooted in Baptism

WHEN MY DAUGHTER ANNALISA WAS BAPTIZED I was so proud to play the role of father that I asked the bishop to come and play the role of pastor. I sat in the pew with my family and let him do everything. When it came time for the baptism, the bishop took the pitcher into his hand and tilted it forward while he prayed, "By the gift of water you nourish and sustain us and all living things." But there was something missing, no sound of water splashing into the basin. A slight mishap, no one had remembered to fill the pitcher with water, and in my role of father, I had not checked it as I would have in my role as pastor. After a poignant silence, the bishop kindly asked, "Does anyone have any water?" We all laughed. Once the water was fetched Annalisa was bathed anew in the life-giving waters of baptism. Later the bishop asked the congregation, "Could this baptism have continued without water? Could we have just pretended?" The answer was no. God chooses tangible means to express grace, such as water, bread, and wine. God connects with us through the ordinary to reveal to us the extraordinary nature of love.

Just as water is central to baptism, baptism is the foundation of confirmation. Confirmation always flows out of baptism. In fact, no scriptures make reference to confirmation, at least not as a separate theological construct or practice. It is rather an implication of baptism, a ministry to help us realize again and again the power and benefits bestowed to us in that original, onetime event. Still, key questions persist:

- How did the practice of confirmation get started?
- Is confirmation as we know it today a continuation of confirmation as the early church knew it?
- How is confirmation related to baptism?
- Who is doing the confirming and what is being confirmed?

The early church understood and practiced confirmation completely different from how it is practiced today. The earliest references are embedded in the initiation rite of baptism in the third century. Essentially one instructional-liturgical initiation rite contained the various parts: prebaptismal instruction, baptism, anointing, sealing, the laying on of hands, admission to the Lord's supper. Not until about A.D. 440 do we have the term *confirmation* being used to describe the episcopal act of confirming baptisms by the bishop, including laying on hands and using oil (chrism) for anointing. The Eastern Orthodox church developed the practice of allowing priests to baptize fully using a chrism (oil) that the bishop had blessed, while the Western Roman church allowed the priest to conduct the water baptism, but reserved the laying on of hands and anointing for the bishop, hence "confirming" and completing the baptism. This confirmation took place periodically, depending on scheduled visits and the availability of the bishop. About A.D. 460, Bishop Faustus of Riez preached on the significance of this episcopal confirmation, claiming that those who received it were more fully Christian. This occasion was the first time confirmation was presented as an additional strengthening of the Holy Spirit over and against the gift bestowed at baptism. Consequently, this understanding of confirmation had immense influence in shaping a new model that became an extension or an expansion of baptism as an independent postbaptismal ritual.

Confirmation as an Expansion of Baptism

Gradually a split occurred and confirmation was seen less as a Spirit gift of strengthening integral to the ongoing significance of baptism and more as an expanded ritual necessary for the approval of an individual's commitment of faith. Scholars suggest that these developments grew out of a variety of factors, including:

- the schism between East and West;
- the need to fight heresies and establish ways for the recent adult convert to verify his or her faithfulness;

- a method to legitimize the authority of papal supremacy.

Eventually, as the Roman church also began to postpone admission to communion and to add an instructional component, the significance of confirmation grew from merely an expansion of baptism to a separate, independent rite. Theologically it came to be considered a necessary rite to complete or fulfill the initial event of baptism.

Confirmation as a Separate Sacrament

In the 12th century, the church took a further step to justify the practice of confirmation as a completion of baptism. In 1150 Archbishop Peter Lombard wrote that baptism gave grace for forgiveness of sin but confirmation through the bishop gave strengthening and perfection for the Christian life. Thomas Aquinas agreed with this view, and in his work *Summa Theologia* he elevated confirmation to a sacrament, totally distinctive from the rite of baptism. However, some in the church disagreed and raised serious concerns over the lack of scriptural authority for confirmation and the lack of evidence for any uniform practice to follow. Still over time the meaning and practice of confirmation evolved away from baptism and led to the official canonization of confirmation as a separate sacrament at the Council of Florence in 1439. This practice implied that confirmation was more important than baptism because the bishop was required to do it and because a greater gift of the Holy Spirit was bestowed. Others saw it as an opportunity to establish a program of educational instruction. Within this context the Reformation movement began and offered a variety of responses to the issue of developing a meaningful practice of confirmation.

The Reformers' Responses

Two major influences, the Bohemian Brethren (1468) and Erasmus of Rotterdam (1466-1536), shifted the liturgical role of confirmation to more of an educational endeavor. They were the building blocks for confirmation as we know it today.

The Bohemian Brethren were the first to further develop confirmation as a way to personally affirm baptism at a later, more mature age. Specific confirmation instruction consistent with the faith confessed at baptism was required. Then, the student was examined to determine whether he or she had accepted the Christian faith and was required to publicly confess his or her intention to remain faithful to promises made at baptism. From there the student was ready to be "confirmed" with the laying on of hands and to receive the prayers and support of the congregation. At this point the confirmand would be acknowledged as a full member of the church and be admitted to the Lord's table.

Erasmus took this approach a step further when he urged for a renewal of the baptismal vow as an obligation for all who have been baptized. He was the first to advocate that the age of puberty is an opportune time when the rite of baptism should be "reenacted," not in the sense of repetition, but as a personal dedication to the vows once spoken at baptism. To accomplish this affirmation, Erasmus proposed a thorough educational program to prepare the child to make a profession of allegiance to Christ and the church. This approach addressed the thorny problem of needing a counterbalance to infant baptism and making a conscious decision to accept the obligations of discipleship and "prove" one's faith. As Frank Klos observed:

Erasmus tried to shift the emphasis in the prevailing doctrine of confirmation from God's gifts to man's obligations to appropriate those gifts, from liturgical rites to catechetical processes.[1]

Because of his contributions, Erasmus is considered to be the founder of catechetical confirmation. He gave birth to the model that continues to shape our understanding of confirmation. The question of whether this model has been beneficial over the centuries remains. Certainly it has led us to regard catechetical instruction for adolescence as a top priority in the church. And yet, has it not also undermined our theological understanding of God's confirming role that begins in baptism and the need to provide catechetical education for all ages? So what was Luther's position on all this?

Martin Luther's Understanding of Confirmation

Let's look at some basic questions:

- Was confirmation Martin Luther's idea?
- What did he actually say about it?
- What was Martin Luther's intention for writing the Small and Large Catechisms?
- Are *confirmation* and *catechism* synonymous?
- Why does confirmation today mainly focus on adolescents?
- Is confirmation a rite of passage into adulthood?
- How did it become like a graduation ceremony?

Luther was not an advocate for a separate confirmation rite. His concern was the need for a daily affirmation of baptism. He was interested in the development of catechetical instruction, but was strongly against any notion that confirmation was necessary to complete baptism. Luther did not regard confirmation as a sacrament commanded by Christ, to which the promises of salvation are attached, such as baptism and Holy Communion. In 1522, Luther voiced concern that confirmation must not become another form of sacramental legalism undermining the graciousness of God's gifts in baptism. Luther said he could support confirmation "as long as it is understood that God knows nothing of it, and has said nothing about it and that what bishops claim for it is untrue."[2]

Luther made a departure from the Roman conception of confirmation as a separate sacrament. Instead, he saw it as a "sacramental ceremony" created by human designs. He insisted that baptism had no need of a bishop to confirm what God has accomplished.

At the same time Luther did support the educational value of the Erasmus model, particularly the development of faith between a child's baptism and the time when they are admitted to the Lord's table. For Luther, catechetical education became a means to link these two sacraments together and to keep the Word alive on a daily basis. This interest led Luther to write the Small and Large Catechisms, which were intended for preparation in receiving Holy Communion and for the ongoing instruction of all Christians, at all ages. In his preface to the Large Catechism Luther calls for a lifelong process of learning:

> Let all Christians exercise themselves in the Catechism daily, and constantly put it into practice....Let them continue to read and teach, to learn and meditate and ponder. Let them never stop until they have proved by experience that they have taught the devil to death and have become wiser than God himself and all his saints....To this end may God grant his grace! Amen.[3]

Other reformers—such as Martin Bucer, Philipp Melanchthon, Johannes Bugenhagen, and Martin Chemnitz—were not as cautious as Luther and took special interest in developing a formalized practice of confirmation for Protestant churches. Experiments to develop an evangelical rite increased and so did the varieties of confirmation. This experimentation led to many of the traditions we find in our current view of confirmation.

Patterns of Confirmation

In order to sort through this historical maze, Arthur Repp in his landmark book, *Confirmation in the Lutheran Church* (1964), organized various types or patterns of confirmation, from the Reformation to the 19th century, into four helpful categories.

Catechetical (Instructional) Confirmation

This prototype of confirmation aimed to be more of an instructional program for admission to the Lord's supper than a full-blown process that culminated with a church rite. Here the influence of Luther and Bugenhagen is predominant. Education was seen as a means to acknowledge one's baptism before receiving the sacrament of Holy Communion. However, it is interesting to note that even after being admitted to the Lord's supper children and adults were expected to continue in their catechetical studies. As Frank Klos points out:

Luther saw this program as an integral part of the church's pastoral and educational ministry to its people....Luther's idea of the lifelong educative process was taking hold. There never was a graduation ceremony short of eternity.[4]

The emphasis was upon instruction, confession of faith, and the prayers of the church. No formalized rites were associated with this approach until the 19th century.

This catechetical method was widely accepted in the Lutheran church, especially in Scandinavia, due to Luther's "father-confessor" Johannes Bugenhagen, who left Wittenberg to bring the principles of the Reformation to Denmark.

Hierarchical (Disciplinary) Confirmation

This pattern of confirmation was also known as the *church discipline model* because it emphasized surrender to Christ in the form of a confession of faith and a vow of obedience to the church. This approach is attributed to Martin Bucer, who is considered to be the father of Lutheran confirmation. Bucer, in 1538, wanted to respond to the Anabaptist charges that Lutherans did not urge personal commitment and lacked an emphasis on moral discipline within the church. As a response to these charges, Bucer's confirmation model really was developed as a polemical device. To him, confirmation gave the opportunity for a vow of loyalty to be confessed after a period of instruction and public examination. This confession of faith was to be followed by the laying on of hands, thus redefining the ancient custom from a Protestant view. Essentially, Bucer took the educational and moral concerns of Erasmus and combined them with Luther's theological and pastoral concerns to shape a public vow of faithfulness to Christ and a pledge of obedience to the traditions of the church. Bucer was also the first to imple-

ment the rite of confirmation as a formal ceremony for admission to Holy Communion.

Eventually from this model, confirmation rather than baptism was understood as the beginning of full-fledged church membership. Confirmation made a major shift to where the emphasis was no longer on the actions of God in baptism and the Spirit's ongoing role to strengthen our discipleship, but upon the individual's vow of commitment and the need for public approval in a onetime rite of passage into adult church membership. Some feel that Bucer went far beyond Luther's understanding that instruction for first communion was just one step in a lifelong catechumenate process.[5] Without a doubt, this model of confirmation has greatly influenced our modern understanding and practice of confirmation as a once-in-a-lifetime rite dependent on human action rather than a lifelong ministry that is of God's doing.

Sacramental Confirmation

This model took Bucer's revived notion of the laying of hands, and the influence of the Roman church, and interpreted the confirmation rite as a signal of a fuller presence of the Holy Spirit and a fuller sense of church membership. It promoted the idea that confirmation, and specifically the blessing of the Holy Spirit, completed baptism, contrary to Luther's position. This approach did not exist independently but was merged into other models to sanction a greater significance to the rite of confirmation and its necessity for full church membership. We can still see this emphasis evident in the church today, whenever the rite itself is regarded as the climax to confirmation ministry.

1963, 1986, 1995   Lutheran World Federation Reports on Confirmation Ministry

1995   *Models of Confirmation and Baptismal Affirmation*

1970   Inter-Lutheran Report on the Theology and Practice of Confirmation

1964   *Confirmation in the Lutheran Church* (Repp)

Confirmation under reconsideration

1675-1785   Confirmation as a conversion experience (Pietistic influence)

Four primary models/influences—
Catechetical

Hierarchical

1440   Confirmation becomes a separate sacrament

Confirmation rooted in baptism

1999 *Confirmation: Engaging Lutheran Foundations and Practices* and *Confirmation: A Congregational Planner*

1998 ELCA Symposium "Confirmation 2000"

1993 Evangelical Lutheran Church in America *Confirmation Ministry Task Force Report*

1969 *Confirmation and Education* (Gilbert)

1968 *Confirmation and First Communion* (Klos)

Efforts to broaden confirmation, return foundation back to baptism, separate first communion from confirmation

1936 *Neubau der Konfirmation* (Doerne)

1700-1850 Confirmation as an academic experience (Rationalistic influence)

Sacramental

Traditional

1536 Confirmation branches out into various practices and meanings in response to the Reformation

Middle Ages Confirmation branches out to become an expansion of baptism

Traditional (Convincing Evidence) Confirmation

This form of confirmation emerged from the desire to maintain the medieval practice without betraying the evangelical principles. This approach was characterized by Philipp Melanchthon's work *Loci Communes* (1543). Here, Melanchthon suggests three components:

- examination of the catechist;

- public confession of faith;

- a special time of prayer for the confirmand accompanied with the laying on of hands.

Melanchthon maintained that confirmation should not be linked to first communion and that any notion of confirmation as a completion of baptism should be rejected. Because of this, Luther generally approved of Melanchthon's model. Another influential figure was Martin Chemnitz (1522-1586). He attempted to develop a new confirmation rite to meld Luther's stress on baptism and the ancient custom of the laying on of hands from a Protestant sense of blessing. He advocated a view of remembering or affirming the covenant of baptism rather than renewing or completing it. From Chemnitz, the most complete confirmation rite from the 16th century is produced: remembrance of baptism (God's action in the baptismal covenant), personal confession of faith, examination of the catechist, admonition to remain faithful and true to the baptismal covenant, and public prayer with the laying on of hands. Chemnitz's stress on a personal confession, examination, and admonition by the church laid the foundation for how confirmation was to be practiced for the next two centuries.

From the Reformation on, the practice and theology of confirmation continued to be shaped by various religious and cultural movements. Arthur Repp identifies two specific influences that have contributed to our current model of confirmation:[6]

Pietistic (Conversion) Confirmation

In 1675 Philipp Spener attempted to find a way to renew and revive the declining church life in Germany. He blamed the rigid orthodoxy of mainline churches for not providing a way to inspire a true experience and testimony of Christian living. He sought a tool to educate children spiritually and give them a significant public ceremony to express their personal commitment. Spener found the catechetical-confirmation practice developed by Bucer to be a perfect vehicle. With an emphasis on personal decision and piety, confirmation became an act of renewal. Catechetical training was redesigned to prepare young persons for a momentous conversion experience, as they would publicly declare their faith to Christ and obedience to the church. This emphasis on conversion changed confirmation into a more subjective, individual affair rather than the concern of the whole community. The value of baptism was found primarily in the covenant or vow that the Christian needed not only to reaffirm, but renew. Soon, in Pietist circles the term *confirmation* was eliminated and replaced by "the renewing of baptismal covenant." Gradually, the significance of baptism diminished, no longer seen as the primary means for full church membership. Instead, true Christian living began when one was confirmed. This model also reinforced the notion that admission to Holy Communion required a public confession of faith at confirmation to verify and validate one's sincerity. Pietism shifted the goal of confirmation as a ministry of receiving and affirming the gifts of God's grace to the personal work of commitment and devotion to Christ.

The influence of Pietism was clearly evident in early American Lutheranism. Henry Melchior Muhlenberg (1711-1787), considered to be one of the founders of Lutheranism in North America, perceived confirmation as an opportunity to awaken faith. He contributed to the 1786 Formula, which served as a guideline for Lutherans in the New World. Confirmation was interpreted as a solemn rite, in which confirmands were asked questions regarding their confession of faith and asked to renew their baptismal vow while pledging their allegiance to the teachings of the church. This emphasis upon heartfelt conversion and feeling renewed played a key role in shaping confirmation theology in America.

Rationalistic (Graduation) Confirmation

A second major influence was driven by cultural values. In part as a reaction against the emotionalism of Pietism and in response to the rise of modern science, rationalism emphasized an academic approach to confirmation. The focus was upon providing young people with the ability to rationally defend their faith and the teachings of the church. As a result, confirmation developed into a kind of graduation ceremony from the church's demanding educational program. Eventually confirmation coincided with the completion of general schooling and the recognition of adult citizenship. In turn, confirmation became more of a cultural rite of passage than a spiritual exercise. Throughout Germany the confirmation rite even became compulsory during the 19th century. The rite was tied to economic and civic privileges and seen as another kind of birthday celebration. This model elevated the role of confirmation to the point that some said it was superior to baptism, and even suggested abolishing baptism.

Fortunately, these proposals left others feeling uneasy, and as the church entered the 20th century, many concerns regarding the practice of confirmation were being raised. All the models or patterns of confirmation listed in preceding text were interwoven and constantly influenced each other, which is why later attempts to reform confirmation presented such a challenge. And yet, as people were willing to explore and reevaluate the historical and theological roots of confirmation, new efforts sprang forth to reconsider confirmation as a ministry by God for the whole church.

Reflection and Discussion Questions

1. What do you think was the original purpose of confirmation? How does it compare with your current understanding and practice of confirmation ministry?

2. In your view, what is confirmation's relation to baptism? To Holy Communion? What do you believe to be the role of the Holy Spirit in confirmation ministry?

3. How did confirmation become associated with the need for a personal confession of faith? Is this component important in your confirmation program? How did confirmation become associated with catechetical instruction and a formal educational program? Is this component important in your confirmation program?

4. What was Luther's view of confirmation? What was he cautious about and what did he endorse? Do you agree with Luther's position?

5. What past influences are still evident in your current practice of confirmation? How do you think these influences continue to shape your approach to confirmation ministry? In a positive way or in a negative way, or both? How do these past influences reinforce or contradict our Lutheran theology and biblical principles, as you understand them?

6. How can our understandings of the history of confirmation help to inform and guide us as we discuss and plan its future?

Notes

1. Frank W. Klos, *Confirmation and First Communion: A Study Book* (Minneapolis: Augsburg Publishing House; Philadelphia: Board of Publication of the Lutheran Church in America; St. Louis: Concordia Publishing House, 1968), 49.

2. "The Estate of Marriage," *Luther's Works*, 45: 24-25.

3. "Luther's Small Catechism," *Book of Concord*, trans. and ed. Theodore G. Tappert (Philadelphia: Fortress Press, 1959), 361.

4. Klos, 57.

5. Ibid., 60.

6. Arthur Repp, *Confirmation in the Lutheran Church* (St. Louis: Concordia Publishing House, 1964), 70-80.

CHAPTER 2

Confirmation in Flux: Studies, Reports, and Redirection

ONCE A WOMAN WHO WAS QUITE DISTRESSED came to my church office. She shared her experience of going through a divorce, battling drug addition, and contemplating suicide. She told me that she used to go to church and remembered being baptized. Then she said, "But I think maybe the cross that was placed on my forehead is gone." After a time of counsel and prayer we went into the sanctuary and stood before the baptismal font. I read from 2 Timothy 1:6-7: "For this reason I remind you to rekindle the gift of God that is within you through the laying on of my hands; for God did not give us a spirit of cowardice, but rather a spirit of power and of love and of self-discipline."

I took water and made the sign of the cross on her forehead and said, "Remember your baptism and remember you are a child of God and belong to God forever." Then I placed my hands on her shoulders and added, "Go forth in the confidence of God's healing Spirit and follow the Spirit's guidance." It was a moment of strengthening, an experience of "confirming" what God has done and promises to do through the power of baptism.

In many respects, with the emphasis on academic achievement and the need to prove one's faith in order to become a full member of the church, the traditional confirmation model lost sight of the central purpose of affirming the power of baptism for discipleship. As many American Lutheran scholars debated the role of confirmation, some felt the key was in writing new catechisms based upon Luther's Small Catechism. Wilhelm Lohe (1872), J. Michael Reu (1904), and Joseph Stump (1907) wrote catechisms in attempts to improve confirmation by developing better instructional materials. However, in general, confirmation became a major source of confusion and contention as people began to ask the same kind of questions that opened this planner:

- What exactly is being confirmed? Baptism? Personal faith? Allegiance to the church?
- What role does the "confession of faith" play?

- Is confirmation an objective or subjective process?

- How is confirmation related to church membership and loyalty to the traditions of the church?

- What is the significance of the laying on of hands?

- How is confirmation related to the Holy Spirit?

- What is the role of the examination?

- What should be the role of the parents?

- What is the appropriate age for confirmation? Should it be limited to only one age group?

- What should the instruction entail?

- How should the catechism be used?

- Should confirmation be linked to Holy Communion?

- Who does the confirming? God? The pastor as God's servant? The confirmand? The congregation?

Significant Studies

These questions sparked new studies, which in turn led to major shifts in understanding and practice. One major contribution to the debate was a German educator, Martin Doerne, who published *Neubau der Konfirmation* (*Rebuilding Confirmation*) in 1936. Doerne proposed a broader understanding of confirmation as a lifelong educational process, constantly providing opportunities to reaffirm and celebrate the promises of baptism. Doerne argued that confirmation should not be linked to the preparation of Holy Communion or understood as a renewal of the baptismal covenant. Rather, confirmation was a reaffirmation of God's grace in baptism and the ongoing process of sanctification through the Spirit and the Word. Doerne's

views were influential upon German and American scholars alike, especially Arthur Repp, who concluded:

> Among other things, [Doerne] noted that the existing practice of confirmation violated a number of Biblical principles and therefore worked against its own success. By allowing confirmation at age 14 to become terminal for the formal religious instruction of the children the church was failing to keep before the mind of its youth and adults the fact that Christian education, in its broader aspects, has no terminal point. Education, he said, must be continuous throughout life, for God desires continually to sanctify His own more fully. Furthermore, Baptism assumes a lifetime of contrition and repentance, and for this the Holy Spirit is to teach the Christian throughout his [or her] life. The church must therefore have an aggressive educational program for its youth for a long time after they have been confirmed.[1]

Unfortunately, Doerne's efforts to reform confirmation, based upon the Reformation's central principles of baptism and grace and the dynamics of Word and Spirit, were largely overlooked during the confusion of the onset of World War II. However, his influence lived on in the various studies and reports that arose in the 1960s and 1970s.

Workshops and seminars on confirmation were initiated worldwide. It was clear that a specific study was needed to offer definition and direction. In 1961 Lutheran World Federation (LWF) engaged in such a study. It was agreed that a concise history of confirmation was needed as well as a survey of how it was actually being practiced.

Arthur Repp took on the research task in his work *Confirmation in the Lutheran Church* (1964). As previously mentioned, Dorne influenced this U.S. scholar. In light of his findings Repp called for a confirmation program grounded in baptism, which

It is within our theological tradition to assert that the Spirit of God confirms us, from conception to consummation. Creation itself is an act of confirmation.

～

Richard Hansen, "Confirmation Yesterday, Today, and Tomorrow," *Dialog*, 36 (1997), 107.

promoted lifelong education to reinforce the constant need for nurture and growth for all members of Christ's body. He recommends:

> Instead of postponing confirmation as long as possible, congregations need to recover the Reformation principle that Christian instruction is to continue after the Christian's first Communion. Confirmation should not be regarded as a sort of temple curtain beyond which the church need not guide and direct the young Christian through further religious instruction. In fact, as with the force and meaning of Baptism, Christian nurture ends only when the sinner-saint is transformed into a Saint of the Church Triumphant. In such a continuing instruction the church assists the Christian in making his [or her] life a coming into his [or her] baptism, helping him [or her] constantly to appropriate the gifts received in the sacrament.[2]

1970 Report

Repp's recommendations are evident in the 1970 report of the Joint Commission on the Theology and Practice of Confirmation, on which he served, and on the two study books that proceeded the commission's report, *Confirmation and Education* (1969), edited by W. Kent Gilbert, and *Confirmation and First Communion: A Study Book* (1968) by Frank W. Klos. Unfortunately both books are no longer available in print. The commission's report also came in response to a survey that was conducted in 1966 called "Current Concepts and Practices of Confirmation in Lutheran Churches." From the tremendous variety in the responses and the gap between an understanding of confirmation versus how it was practiced, the commission decided to develop a churchwide study program. The major elements that emerged for reconsideration and reform included separating confirmation from first communion (rec-

ommending an earlier admission age), the desire to dispel the notion that confirmation was a completion of baptism, and that full membership happened at confirmation, not baptism. Also, quoting from Repp, the commission recommended that "the heart of confirmation lies in the instruction of the Word, not in the rite that precedes it.…[and that confirmation] is only one step in a lifelong continuum of Christian growth and education."[3] The report also offered a new definition of confirmation as a

> …pastoral and educational ministry of the church that is designed to help baptized children identify with the life and mission of the adult Christian community and that is celebrated in a public rite.[4]

After the commission studied the responses of the congregations, it modified the definition by adding "to help the baptized through Word and Sacrament" and omitted the word *adult* and any mention of a public rite. These subtle changes make clear that nurture and growth through word and sacrament is essential in confirmation, as pastoral and educational ministry, while the need for a public rite is not essential. Confirmation involves the whole Christian community in its purpose of baptismal identity and mission. For the first time in hundreds of years confirmation is lifted up as a process rather than an event, a ministry rather than a rite. In addition the report recommends giving greater responsibility to lay leadership, especially parents and sponsors. In fact, confirmation has to do with the total life of a congregation and its priorities for pastoral and educational ministry. Not only did this report and study guides help to separate confirmation from first communion, it also reidentified confirmation as "Affirmation of Baptism" (as presented in *Lutheran Book of Worship*, 1978) rather than a renewal or reactivation of a baptismal covenant.

1993 Task Force Report

Recently the Evangelical Lutheran Church in America presented a new effort to underscore some of the primary reforms of the 1970 *Report*. The *Confirmation Ministry Task Force Report*, adopted by the ELCA Churchwide Assembly in 1993, relied heavily upon the 1970 revised definition and identified a focal question for its study: "What is the role of the congregation in affirming youth in Christian faithfulness with an emphasis on lifelong learning and discipleship?"[5]

In many ways this question is reminiscent of the same concerns raised by Doerne, Repp, Klos, and the 1970 commission report; namely how can confirmation, as an affirmation of baptism, be a lifelong process rather than a once-in-a-lifetime event? And how can confirmation ministry be designed so that it promotes Christian faithfulness with lifelong learning and discipleship according to the needs of the whole congregation? The task force also called for a "gospel-centered and grace-centered" vision of confirmation ministry, with less stress on needing to achieve just the right formula of instruction. The report states:

> Confirmation ministry is an opportunity for congregations to renew the vision of living by grace, grounded in Baptism. This vision is especially important for ministry with young Christians, but it also has lifelong implications.[6]

In general, the task force reiterated the centrality of baptism and its dynamic power in shaping our sense of identity/community, mission/discipleship, and vocation/ministry. In addition, with this understanding of "the lifelong nature of God's act in Baptism and the continuous need for God's Word of grace," the task force concluded that confirmation ministry is more than education for youth. Reaffirming Luther's position, the task force instead focused attention on "the baptismal experience of dying and rising to new life with Christ [to be] experienced daily."[7] Also offered is the invitation to lifelong learning and a confirmation curriculum that focuses on learning moments, such as transitions in life, at all ages, to help members return to their baptism and see these experiences in light of God's grace. Likewise, the task force suggested a provision for a variety of repeatable baptismal affirmation rites at significant times within the life cycle. Some examples include moving into a nursing home, beginning parenthood or grandparenthood, choosing or changing an occupation, moving out of the parental home, the diagnosis of a chronic illness, the end of one's first year of mourning, the ending of a relationship, and retirement.[8] In some cases these rites of affirmation would entail catechetical instruction, or supportive learning groups, or a relationship with a mentor, all to provide opportunities for study and reflection. The task force concluded its report by stating that these rites of affirmation of baptism should have certain characteristics. They should be:

- evangelical (displaying and proclaiming the grace, love, justice, and beauty of God);

- baptismal (linked with Baptism in word, symbol, action, and timing);

- honest (reflecting the experience, beliefs, and context of those making affirmation, and placed within the faith of the whole church);

- communal (involving as much of the community as feasible, in both planning and celebration);

- voluntary (assuring willing, not coerced, participants);

- contextual (reflecting a sensitivity to the cultural context, history, and piety of the congregation).[9]

The task force also offered a number of suggestions for implementing an effective confirmation ministry in congregations. Clearly, foremost is their recommendation to "create, or designate, [or identify] a confirmation ministry team to give shape and direction to the planning and coordination of pastoral and educational confirmation ministry."[10] The task force recognized and stressed the key role that leadership plays, which includes both clergy and laity, in any effective program of ministry.

Finally, the 1993 task force calls on synods, the churchwide organization, seminaries, and publishing houses to be in partnership with congregations in developing a broad variety of support resources, such as materials, networks, and trained leaders for confirmation ministry.[11] Variety, creativity, flexibility, partnership, and cooperation seem to be common themes when talking about the type of resources needed for a broader, more inclusive approach to confirmation ministry. These themes are especially important when we face the challenge of making confirmation intergenerational, intercultural, international, and hopefully one day soon even interdenominational, as we affirm together our common baptismal promises.

1995 Lutheran World Federation Study

These concerns are well outlined in the Lutheran World Federation 1995 global report titled "Confirmation Ministry Study" (LWF Documentation 38). This study emphasizes the fact that confirmation is a ministry that must be dynamic and open to ever-changing contexts and needs. With the concern of a constantly growing number of people absent from any congregational life, this study asks important questions about how confirmation ministry can address both current and future realities that face the church. Four themes emerge:

- The overall mission of the congregation plays a key role in shaping confirmation ministry. The more we understand that all elements of ministry are interconnected, the better the church is able to serve the community as a whole.

- Confirmation ministry and youth education are most effective when they are practiced as a part of a lifelong journey. Youth education thrives when adult education is strong. Confirmation ministry is broadening to include numerous affirmations of baptism, which occur over a lifetime.

- Programs designed specific to the congregation's context are to be encouraged. The best resources are those that are adapted to the needs of the families and students involved in the community. This design concern includes programs that keep the parent's needs in mind and encourage their full participation.

- Partnership between the congregation and the confirmation students must be reinforced. The Christian identity of the young person as it contributes to the identity of the community is central to the process of affirming one's baptism.[12]

In addition to the LWF study, the book *Models of Confirmation and Baptismal Affirmation* (1995), by Robert Browning and Roy Reed, examines current trends in the practice of confirmation ministry in seven major U.S. denominations. The study suggests that if this practice is to continue as an important ministry for the church a broader understanding of confirmation ministry must be developed, based upon a dynamic view of baptism, discipleship, renewal of commitment, and a celebration of what God does through grace. Browning and Reed identify major shifts or trends that are reshaping confirmation liturgically,

The very sustenance of life is a matter of God's confirming action.

⌐

Richard Hansen, "Confirmation Yesterday, Today, and Tomorrow," *Dialog*, 36 (1997), 107.

theologically, and educationally. Many of their findings support the recommendations of the 1970 and 1993 Lutheran reports:

- Baptism, not confirmation, lies at the heart of conversion and commitment. Confirmation is not another initiation rite; it neither completes nor lessens baptism. Our theology of baptism must inform and direct our theology of confirmation ministry.

- Liturgies that inspire commitment and foster an ongoing baptismal ministry are needed. Repeatable baptismal affirmations must transcend age or time, and reinforce lifelong learning and discipleship.

- The eucharist is the climactic moment of Christian initiation, just as it was for the early church in the "unified initiation" practice.

- Christian initiation and baptismal affirmation are communal experiences, not just for the individual alone. The Holy Spirit is never reserved as private affair, but a gift to the whole community.

- A new movement in the church stresses education, not as indoctrination but as an honest quest for the truth that integrates all of life.

- The move toward a faith development perspective includes persons of all ages in the confirmation process, not just youth and children. Catechetical instruction must be responsive to a creative integration between life and faith. No longer can the traditional schooling method serve as the primary strategy for Christian education, but an approach that draws from the all the various resources within and without the community of faith.

- Worship life, education, and service are no longer held as separate entities, but as interrelated and to be practiced in harmony. Learning must be interdisciplinary and based in practice not just theory.

- Catechetical instruction is integrated with spirituality and the importance of all our various relationships: parents, peers, teachers, mentors, sponsors, the congregation, and the world. Partnerships in mutual learning are being affirmed as confirmation ministry is shaped by a team approach.[13]

Browning and Reed make a compelling case that each of these new trends in confirmation ministry can be related to the overriding shift of making confirmation a repeatable experience designed to remind believers of the power and importance of baptism as they face various life transitions and decisions. The focus is upon God's ongoing work of the Spirit to confirm or strengthen our faith and commitment through the grace given to us in the sacraments of Holy Baptism and Holy Communion and the word. This view clearly reflects Luther's theology and the principles of the Reformation, as the *Book of Concord* affirms:

> Confirmation is to be seen as a sanctifying exercise of baptismal faith, which works at the completion of what God has already begun and continues in baptism.…[It] does require daily acts of faith which will allow God to grant an experiential confirmation to that faith again and again until the ultimate confirmation occurs in the resurrection on the last day.[14]

(For a further in-depth study of the historical and theological developments within confirmation ministry see *Confirmation: Engaging Lutheran Foundations and Practices*, chapter 3, "Lutheran Confirmation Ministry in a Historical Perspective," and chapter 4, "The Theology of Confirmation.")

Reflection and Discussion Questions

1. In relation to your congregation's confirmation program, "What is the role of the congregation in affirming youth in Christian faithfulness with an emphasis on lifelong learning and discipleship?" (1993 task force question).

2. What is your response to the statement "confirmation is a process rather than a onetime event, a ministry rather than a public rite"? What changes would have to occur in your congregation to adapt to this understanding of confirmation?

3. What is your response to the claim that confirmation should include repeatable baptismal affirmations for all people, at all ages? How does this view compare with your current practice of confirmation ministry?

4. How is your congregation involved in developing the vision and implementing the practice of confirmation ministry? Who is responsible? What is the role of the pastor, the parents, the students, the Christian education committee, and the whole congregation? What difference would the establishment of a "confirmation team" make within your congregation?

5. What is unique about your congregation's identity that should inform and shape the practice of confirmation ministry? How would you describe the context or local setting of your congregation (for example, the neighborhood, economic, cultural, and family dynamics)? How do you take these factors into account as you design your confirmation ministry?

Notes

1. Luther E. Lindberg and Ralph W. Holmin, *Confirmation and Education*, W. Kent Gilbert, ed. (Philadelphia: Fortress Press, 1969), 18.

2. Arthur Repp, *Confirmation in the Lutheran Church* (St. Louis: Concordia Publishing House, 1964), 167.

3. Frank W. Klos, *Confirmation and First Communion: A Study Book* (Minneapolis: Augsburg Publishing House; Philadelphia: Board of Publication of the Lutheran Church in America; St. Louis: Concordia Publishing House, 1968), 185.

4. Ibid., 6.

5. *Confirmation Ministry Task Force Report* (ELCA, 1993), 1.

6. Ibid., 5.

7. Ibid., 9.

8. Ibid., 10.

9. Ibid.

10. Ibid., 14.

11. Ibid.

12. LWF, *Confirmation: A Study Document*, 41.

13. Robert L. Browning and Roy H. Reed, *Models of Confirmation and Baptismal Affirmation* (Birmingham: Religious Education Press, 1995), 29-50.

14. As paraphrased from the *Book of Concord* by Theodore R. Jungkuntz, *Confirmation and the Charismata* (Lanhan, Md.: University Press of America, 1983), 52.

CHAPTER 3

Where Do We Go from Here?
New Directions in
Confirmation Ministry

THE SIGN ON THE DOOR SAID "Sterile environment: Don't enter without washing." It was a room specially designed to keep out germs, for an infant without an immune system. I put on the green gown and, covered from head to toe, entered the room. All I could see of the parents were their eyes. Kristina lay motionless inside the incubation tube. Her red face against the white sheets, she had her eyes open too. I carried water in a plastic bowl; the nurse had given her approval. I wondered if we should sing a song or something, but the silence before we prayed was quite sufficient. I reached through the little portal opening, and even with gloves I could feel Kristina's soft and warm forehead. Three times I spilled the water, on the floor, on the sheets, and on the little girl who gently moved toward my hand. I pronounced, "In the name…," and the room was no longer sterile. Tears flowed alongside the water I placed on the parents' foreheads to remind them of whose they were. And the mother said to me, "Tonight I will finally sleep."

Luther once said that the role of the water and the Word is "to break the huge and solid wall that surrounds the heart, which is at the center of our humanness."[1] To approach confirmation as a lifelong and comprehensive ministry is an attempt to emphasize what God continues to do through our baptism. Yet, the key question we face today is how to work in harmony with God. What models or approaches should we use? What kind of resource tools will we need? And who is going to develop, implement, and evaluate these new models and resources? Even though we have evidence that our understanding of confirmation is expanding, a recent survey showed that confirmation is still practiced in most Lutheran congregations in accordance with past historical models:

- 67 percent say they have not changed the basic approach in several years;

- 79 percent focus confirmation ministry entirely on those in eighth and ninth grades;

- 95 percent primarily use the Small Catechism;

- 92 percent feel that it is the pastor's job to plan out and be the primary confirmation instructor;

- 62 percent have weekly instructional classroom sessions;

- 83 percent of congregations offer confirmation independent of other congregations.

One more statistic that has continued is the large dropout rate by youth after the confirmation rite is completed. Only 46 percent of the congregations report that a majority of those confirmed remain active in the congregation.[2] Certainly many factors surround this statistic, but clearly it is the driving force behind many of the new attempts to redesign confirmation ministry that have emerged during the last few years.

Models of Confirmation Ministry

The 1993 ELCA Confirmation Ministry Task Force lifted up six models of effective confirmation ministry programs.

- *Longer and Later* includes young people from early childhood through high school years.

- *Meeting of Young People* emphasizes conversation and supportive small groups for learning; features one to two years of intensive work.

- *The Confirming Community* encourages relationships between confirmands and older youth or adults who serve as mentors and tutors.

- *The Catechumenal Parish* builds on the historic catechumenal process, a journey ritually marked by the whole congregation.

- *The Renewed School* focuses on classroom activities and the teacher's role as mentor.

- *Vow-Driven Catechesis* builds on the vow made at confirmation and five projects.

These six models are further developed in Ken Smith's booklet *Six Models of Confirmation Ministry* (1993).[3]

Recent discussions with ELCA congregations around the country reveal a growing diversity confirmation ministry practices. Amid considerable variation and diversity the current approaches to confirmation ministry fall into seven categories:

- Classroom (Traditional)

- Classroom (Experiential)

- Expanded

- Large group presentation/Small group discussion

- Individualized

- Home-based schooling

- Retreat

The chart on page 26 identifies the primary characteristics and typical activities employed by congregations using a particular approach. The "approach" describes the predominate feature of the congregation's confirmation ministry, but does not exclude other elements. For example, a congregation that uses the traditional classroom approach may use retreating or assignments to be completed with family to enhance the confirmation experience. Other elements such as mentoring, community service, music, involvement in worship, congregation committee work, and so on work well with any of the approaches.

All these different styles or approaches to confirmation are exceptional examples of current efforts to reform confirmation ministry to address the needs of youth and

Confirmation Ministry in the Congregation

Approach	Primary Characteristics	Typical Activities
Classroom (Traditional)	Study of the Bible and Small Catechism for junior high or middle school students.	Lecture, reading assignments, memory work, tests.
Classroom (Experiential)	Examine life experiences in light of the Bible, the Catechism, and Lutheran history and heritage.	Active, experiential approach that allows students to explore the connection between their experience and traditional Lutheran texts (Bible and Catechism) and theology.
Expanded (This is often called "Longer and Later.")	Lutheran faith formation for youth in grades 1-12. Study of Lutheran history, heritage, and texts (Bible and Small Catechism) for youth in grades 1-12.	Supplemental classes in Sunday school, family classes at key points (first communion and distribution of Bibles) in a child's life. Retreats and service projects of high school youth. Often includes a more traditional two-year period of study for junior high or middle school youth.
Large group presentation/ Small group discussion	Presentation of program content with opportunity for young people to explore the intersection of faith and life in small group discussion.	Creative and engaging large group presentation followed by small group discussion led by volunteers.
Individualized	Study of the Bible and Small Catechism for junior high or middle school students.	Students work through a prescribed curriculum at their own pace. Adults may be present to answer questions or to provide occasional small group experiences.
Home-based schooling	Study of the Bible and Small Catechism for junior high or middle school students.	Resources and instructions for their use are sent into the homes where parents or guardians participate with their children in the completion of the course of study.
Retreat	Study of the Bible and Small Catechism or an experiential opportunity for junior high or middle school students to explore the intersection of faith and life in a concentrated community experience.	An integrated community (family) experience that includes worship, study, play, meals, and time for reflection.

their families. Some have broadened the scope of confirmation ministry to include adult mentors, lay teachers, cooperation with other congregations, more home-based education, and starting with children at an early age. Still others maintain that if we are to communicate to youth that confirmation is not graduation, we need to develop confirmation models that incorporate lifelong learning throughout the ongoing journey of baptismal affirmation.

Symposium "Confirmation 2000"

Both the problems and the opportunities of confirmation ministry were discussed at the Symposium "Confirmation 2000" held in June 1998. Pastors, educators, lay leaders, camp directors, and churchwide staff came together for three days to envision the future of confirmation ministry. Of particular concern were the results of a recent churchwide survey, asking why a majority of those who were recently confirmed have not remained actively involved in the congregation. A recurring theme in the survey responses was the desire for more educational experiences before and after the traditional confirmation rite and the need to foster bonds of lifelong commitment and discipleship. For many, confirmation still felt like a graduation from church and a rite of passage that, once completed, signals the end to all learning. This sense was amplified by the statistic that nearly 75 percent of adults in the Lutheran church never participate in any kind of educational endeavor after finishing confirmation. The symposium participants discussed how to create programs that connect baptismal affirmation to daily living and to the transitions of life, not just adolescence. Special attention was given to the recommendation of the 1993 task force to include repeatable baptismal

affirmations that promote faith formation for the whole people of God at every opportunity. In addition, it was agreed that the catechism is too important to be limited only to children and youth. Instead, we need to find ways to make confirmation ministry inclusive and contextual so that learning and discipleship is a goal for the overall mission of the congregation.

At the symposium, four basic strategies were developed to help guide congregations to assess what needs to occur for confirmation to continue as a viable ministry of the church in the 21st century:

Vision

What are our theological and educational values and practices for confirmation ministry? We may need to "re-language" and "rethink" what we are doing, just as the church did when communion was separated from confirmation. The hope of this planner; the textbook, *Confirmation: Engaging Lutheran Foundations and Practices*; the 1993 *Task Force Report*; and the Division for Congregational Ministries (DCM) booklet, *Confirmation: More Than Just Business as Usual!* is to enable the church to communicate and shape its vision for confirmation ministry by better understanding its history and the richness of our theological and educational traditions. It will be the task of both individual congregations engaged in conversation and the church in general at seminaries, colleges, and synod and churchwide assemblies.

Resources

A variety of resources of all types, including people, print, video, and electronic, need to be developed according to the needs determined by the congregational confirmation ministry team and in partnership with publishing houses and other strategic alliances. What needs to be the primary

The goal of confirmation is to help individuals "clarify what they believe themselves at a particular point on their faith journey."

Richard Osmer, "Reconstructing Confirmation," *Theology Today*, 49 (1), 64.

curriculum? It is interesting to note that in the April survey more than 40 percent of congregations said they develop their own curriculum. The need for resources that guide a lifelong approach to baptismal affirmation is crucial if a broader understanding of confirmation is actually to be practiced.

Training or Leadership

Workshops and training events must be offered for confirmation teams to equip team members to provide leadership in shaping and implementing a new vision for confirmation ministry. Effective leadership within the national church office, synod offices, educational institutions, and congregations is crucial to train teachers and promote participation and ownership of a vision for vital confirmation ministry by church members.

Networking

Congregations and leaders need to be connected in order to share new ideas and experiences that will help to provide timely and relevant information. Through telephone, Internet, newsletters, or virtual networks, a sense of partnership needs to be fostered between congregations, churchwide staff, publishing houses, seminaries, and even other church denominations. Guidance, whether for theological perspectives or for practical suggestions, needs to be readily accessible for everyone.

How can these four strategies be helpful to your congregation's vision of confirmation ministry? How can they be used to implement a confirmation ministry that promotes the grace of baptism, the value of catechesis, and the freedom of affirmation ceremonies? Who will provide the leadership? What resources will you rely on? How are you connected to other sources of information and guidance?

The symposium participants saw clearly that Lutherans do not have one single consistent church practice or pattern for confirmation ministry. This fact was not identified as a problem, but as an opportunity to better understand how the Spirit strengthens Christian identity, vocation, ministry, and discipleship. The future hope of confirmation ministry may be found in a diversity of approaches and content. Exciting and creative programs are appearing all the time. Each has a unique way to develop confirmation ministry, participating with the Spirit to reinforce and empower baptismal faith through education and discipleship.

This perspective leads us to our final chapter and the attempt to share some guidelines that will help you discern your congregation's current strengths and future needs. These directives will enable you to plan a confirmation ministry program that is related to your own particular context and yet grounded in our Lutheran theological heritage. As Luther claimed, confirmation is simply "monkey-business" if it becomes a rigid program, separated from the richness of God's grace and the Spirit's leading.[4] Jesus tells us the Spirit is like the wind; nobody understands just how or where it will blow (John 3:8). Our challenge is to honor the Spirit's integrity by being flexible and open, willing to try new approaches and adapt to new directions. At Pentecost the Spirit demonstrates the power that comes from embracing diversity and learning to communicate in many languages, yet being united in the one gospel of Christ. The goal of the Spirit is to promote communication, and communication opens the door to communion with God and each other. As we consider the future of confirmation ministry, we have an opportunity to listen and trust the Spirit's leading and to journey in a mutual endeavor.

Reflection and Discussion Questions

1. How active are your youth after they "complete" confirmation? Why do you think some remain active? Why do others decide not to? What should the church do to keep youth and young adults active in congregational life? How can we help them to comprehend baptismal affirmation as a lifelong process?

2. Have you used any of the various approaches described in this chapter? Which have proven to be most effective, and least effective? Why? Which new approach sounds attractive to consider?

3. What curriculum resources do you currently use? How would do you assess their value?

4. What kind of overall resources would be most helpful to you? How does your congregation network with others for information, resources, ideas, and support in confirmation ministry? What kind of leadership training does your congregation provide for the ministry of confirmation? What kind of training would you like to see seminaries, churchwide, and synod staffs provide?

5. What do you think about the suggestion of a lifelong approach to confirmation ministry, with catechism instruction and repeatable baptismal affirmations offered for all ages throughout the life cycle? How would this approach change the way you understand and practice confirmation ministry in you congregation? What would need to happen for your congregation to implement this approach? What kind of resources would you need?

Notes

1. *Luther's Works*, 26: 310.

2. *Confirmation Ministry Questionnaire* (ELCA Department for Research and Evaluation, April 1998).

3. Ken Smith, *Six Models of Confirmation Ministry* (Chicago: Evangelical Lutheran Church in America, Division for Congregational Ministries, 1993).

4. "The Estate of Marriage," *Luther's Works*, 45: 24.

CHAPTER 4

Guiding Steps for the Baptismal Journey of Confirmation Ministry

IT IS THE BAPTISM OF OUR LORD. A new year and an opportunity for new beginnings. Little Andrew David has just been baptized. Now the junior high confirmation class is invited to come forward to participate in an affirmation of baptism ceremony. Lauren is excited and nervous as she comes forward to the altar rail. She feels good about all she has learned in the past three years in the "Baptismal Life" group. The program was really a lot of fun, but it took a major commitment of time attending the retreats and monthly learning events with other churches. But she made a lot of new friends. She smiles as she sees her adult mentor come forward with her parents beside her. But the next sight makes her smile even bigger. It is her grandmother, Evelyn, coming forward to kneel beside Lauren and join in affirming her own baptism. She has just completed a yearlong program that involved a baptismal support group like her own. Her grandmother's group focused on learning to care for an ailing spouse. Her grandfather had a stroke about two years ago.

Other adults come forward who belong to different "Baptismal Life" groups, sometimes called *affinity groups* because they are organized around what people share in common. Lauren holds her grandmother's hand as the pastor places her hands upon their shoulders and says a prayer. She then makes the sign of the cross on their foreheads with oil. Lauren senses a certain comfort as she affirms the Spirit's presence and knows that God's confirming grace will give her a renewed confidence for facing the challenges of high school. Yes Lauren feels thankful, but she is even more thankful to know that this moment isn't the end, only another new beginning.

Affirming confirmation as a lifelong baptismal ministry is a significant way to strengthen current efforts to provide a vital program for the youth of our church. The youth will be encouraged to see adults living out their faith, becoming active participants in confirmation ministry. Youth will also begin to understand that baptismal affirmation and spiritual development is a lifelong venture.

It is clear from a recent survey that for the majority of Lutheran congregations confirmation is a primary form of youth ministry and faith formation for children. A lifelong approach to confirmation ministry will incorporate this traditional priority of the Spirit's work and ministry to and with the adolescent members of our church as a vital stepping stone in building a foundation for baptismal living. The excellent opportunity confirmation provides to emphasize the church's concern for youth and to equip them for their unique baptismal journey needs to continue. However, specific guidelines need to be established to assure that the programs we offer are gospel-centered and grace-centered, both in content and in approach, while being sensitive to the needs of the youth within the congregation's particular context. One of the first tasks the confirmation ministry team faces is to agree upon the priorities that will guide the planning process so that a lifetime of learning isn't crammed into a two- or three-year time span. Secondly, tools are needed in order to regularly evaluate current confirmation programs to see whether they provide the pastoral and educational ministry geared to enable our youth to become lifelong disciples of Christ.

Step One: Setting Priorities

The 1993 *Task Force Report* identified three major themes that proceed from baptism. These basic goals can help to discern your priorities as you plan an approach to confirmation ministry among youth as it relates to the overall plan for parish education.

Identity/Community

Baptism reveals our identity as God's children, forgiven and renewed, members of Christ's body. Because it comes from God's action, this identity takes precedence over other aspects of who we are: ethnic background, gender, nationality, class, or culture. These aspects are not denied; rather they are claimed for Christ and God's mission to the world. Confirmation ministry is an important opportunity for young Christians to reflect upon their identity as Christians within the baptized community and the world.

Mission/Discipleship

Baptism involves us in Christ's mission, through the church, to bring the gospel to all people. Confirmation ministry can inspire young Christians to become an active participant in this mission by becoming faithful disciples, or followers of Christ. We rely upon word and sacrament, worship and prayer, study and conversation to sustain and direct our life as disciples.

Vocation/Ministry

Baptism evokes our calling or vocation to service and daily ministry. Youth especially face far-reaching decisions about education, marriage or singleness, citizenship, and occupation. Confirmation ministry addresses this time of decision making. It can empower young people to trust their own experiences of Christ's faithfulness as they identify values and beliefs to which they commit their lives. Confirmation can help young Christians determine how they want to live now and in the future.

A primary question throughout this planner has been how confirmation ministry can be integrated into the overall goal of your congregation's educational and pastoral ministry. Some also ask, how is the task of confirmation ministry any different from the task of Christian education in general? How can we differentiate between the two if we pursue confirmation as a means to lifelong learning? It would be nice if we could make a clear distinction, but often our attempts have led to a definition and practice of confirmation as a program that concerns only adolescence. Instead, these foundational themes will help you to structure a program that can be unique for youth while reinforcing the fact that these basic issues remain at the heart of our baptismal ministry at every stage of life. The recent statement on the practice of word and sacrament makes this point clear.

> The parish education of the congregation is part of its baptismal ministry. Indeed, all the baptized require life-long learning, the daily re-appropriation of the wonderful gifts given in Baptism.[1]

Once specific guiding principles are agreed upon and organized, the confirmation ministry team will be able to develop and clearly publicize a mission statement for confirmation ministry as it relates to the entire congregation. It will become possible to identify what confirmation ministry attempts to accomplish in particular to youth and explore creative ways to integrate it with other congregational ministries. These three guidelines can help you shape a comprehensive program that is both sensitive to the goal of faith formation for our youth and incorporates a sense of partnership throughout the baptized community.

Step Two: Assessing Your Current Program

These three primary themes can also help you develop an assessment tool for evaluating your current confirmation program. (See also "Confirmation Ministry Assessment Tool," page 46, for another assessment tool.)

Identity/Community

- How are we identifying young people's issues and needs? Are we communicating the gospel (God's forgiveness and saving grace) in a language they understand and relate to? Are we teaching youth how to learn, giving them the tools to ask questions and search for answers for themselves?

- Are we asking youth, parents, and adults what they want and expect from our confirmation ministries?

- What elements of our program are meeting needs and expectations? How can we build on them?

- Does our current program emphasize and convey grace?

- How does our current program strengthen the baptismal identity of being a child of God?

- How does our program incorporate the Bible and Luther's Small Catechism as key resources for understanding one's identity and relationships? How do we help participants to understand what it means to be a Christian? What it means to be a Lutheran?

- How does our program support parents and siblings as they share in the goals of confirmation ministry?

- How do we engage other adults to serve as examples of faith for our youth?

- How does our program communicate baptismal formation as a process, not an end in itself? A vital step in the lifelong baptismal journey and not a graduation ceremony out of the church?

- How does our program enhance the youth's relationship among peers? Youth from other churches?

- How does our program foster a sense of belonging to the baptized community, both locally and globally?

Mission/Discipleship

- Are we training youth to use the disciplines of faith, such as daily devotion through God's word, prayer, and worship? How do we help them to use these disciplines to make decisions about their lives?

- Are we actively including youth in the overall mission of our congregation?

- Do we provide specific opportunities for youth to participate in the varied ministries of our church?

- How do we inspire and instruct youth to proclaim the gospel in their daily lives? Do they know how to share their faith story?

- Do youth invite their friends to attend confirmation events? What would need to change so that they would want to invite their friends?

- Does our current program evoke a sense of joy over one's baptism and the ongoing power of grace?

- Are we making the Bible and the Small Catechism accessible by using relevant modes of communication and being sensitive to various cultural perspectives?

- Do we include youth and parents in planning the confirmation program? Do they have a sense of ownership in the development of the program?

- Do we provide in-home resources to promote a partnered sense of learning and spiritual development for families?

- How are our congregation's education and worship ministries working to provide a mutual support of confirmation ministry?

- What types of worship rites do we use to celebrate baptismal affirmation? How do they mark endings and beginnings? How are they connected to life's transitions? How do they affirm a strengthening of baptismal faith to face new challenges?

- Do we offer retreats, camping experiences, and cooperative learning events with other churches to broaden our approach to learning and spiritual growth?

Vocation/Ministry

- Does our program promote a sense of calling for our youth to ministry and service through the gift of baptism?

- Does our pastoral and lay leadership in confirmation ministry provide a positive role model of vocation and ministry to our youth?

- Does our program engage youth in community service where they can put what they are learning into action?

- Does our program reinforce the baptismal calling for our young people to serve as ministers in daily life?

- Do we provide opportunities for our young people to experience and reflect upon God's world of diverse cultures and variety of ethnic backgrounds and faith expressions?

- How does our program help youth to identify and share their spiritual gifts? How does our congregation help youth to recognize and use their God-given talents for the benefit of the church's ministry?

- Does our program help youth to identify vocational and personal aspirations and offer support in helping them to make significant decisions in life?

- Do we look to youth to be partners in ministry to the children within our congregation, providing positive role models of faith and caring?

- Does our program allow young people to struggle with social issues in light of the gospel and baptismal faith? Are they encouraged to participate in social justice concerns and advocacy ministry?

Step Three: Design and Implementation of Your Plan

These foundational goals can also serve as a framework for developing specific steps to address the particular spiritual development needs for youth and their families. Here are a few practical examples of how congregations might design and implement a plan according to these goals:

Identity/Community

- Ask the youth to keep a prayer journal. Parents also are given a prayer journal and asked to write down their prayers for their youth. Around Thanksgiving have youth put up a "graffiti prayer wall" and ask members to share their prayers of Thanksgiving. During Lent put up another one and ask people to share prayers of confession and concern. Coincide the activity with a study on prayer, using examples from the Bible, Luther, and other inspirational figures.

- Have the youth pass out candles and seashells to every member on The Baptism of Our Lord Sunday. Share a plan that the youth help develop for the congregation to celebrate baptismal anniver-saries throughout the new year. The seashells can be filled with water, placed alongside the candle in the bathroom, and serve as a daily reminder of God's baptismal grace. Have youth conduct a survey on what baptism means for daily life and ministry. Discuss results in light of Luther's understanding of baptism.

- Have the youth select adult mentors. Ask youth to help prepare a job description and an invitation that is given to the adults who have been selected. Once a month after regular confirmation classes, invite mentors to join the youth for dinner and time of worship. Mentors also attend field trips. Youth and mentor schedule individual sessions together, perhaps visiting a shut-in or preparing a meal for a local food program.

- Examine and adapt the ancient rite of the catechumenate into your confirmation program. *Catechumenate* means a "sounding" or "resounding," as when the word of God resounds in the heart of a believer. Youth participate in a specially designed catechesis, which enables them to undergo a process of faith formation through education and worship. An emphasis is placed on baptismal living as it is guided by the spiritual disciplines of prayer, worship, scripture reading, and daily ministry.

- Begin confirmation ministry in kindergarten with basic memory work. Hand out a daily devotional to all the families. Invite parents or guardians to attend special learning events to train them to be faithful spiritual leaders for their children. Practical help for in-home worship, Bible study, and catechism instruction is provided. The parents participate in a confirmation-commissioning worship service to affirm their role as spiritual guides. Also provide instruction and encouragement to baptismal sponsors.

- Develop a baptismal ministry program that incorporates and nurtures the stages of life and faith development. Beginning with pre-birth to facing the reality of death, offer catechetical instruction through support groups, in-home resources, and experiential learning events customized to fit each life transition. Offer baptismal affirmation celebrations throughout the seasons of life and faith.

- Link up with other area churches and organize a monthly learning event for confirmands. Events could include field trips to a mortuary, birthing center, prison, nursing home, local synagogue, mosque, or Buddhist temple. Learning themes could focus on issues of particular interest to youth: relationships, peer pressure, race relations, environment, sexuality and love, parents and family dynamics. Use small and large group dynamics for discussion and presentations. Location of events will rotate between congregations. Prepare follow-up activities for at home or in local congregations.

Mission/Discipleship

- On Rally Day in September have youth hand out Luther's Small Catechism to every member. Develop a plan to have the whole congregation study and celebrate Luther's words of wisdom and our Lutheran heritage. Throughout the year have youth members lead various events, seminars, and worship experiences around what they have learned from the Small Catechism (plan a Reformation Food Party, do a chancel drama, host a baptismal pool party). Prepare in-home resources for further study and enrichment on how this document serves as a mission statement for our church and our lives.

- Have youth make a video asking children and adults about the mission of the church and what it means to be a follower of Jesus. Host a special "Discipleship Dinner" and show the video. Share the mission statement for confirmation ministry in light of the congregation's mission statement.

- Develop individualized projects for each youth in confirmation. Projects could include a "scripture" project, a "faith/life" project, and a "baptism/worship" project. Create ways to share these projects with the entire congregation.

- Make worship a central experience of confirmation. Use different modes of worship and invite youth to help create their own worship services. Invite youth to take an active role in Sunday worship. Celebrate Holy Communion or Affirmation of Baptism throughout and as an integral part of classtime or learning events.

- Have youth participate in first communion instruction classes. Invite youth to serve as mentors to the children involved and create a "buddy system" for the sake of discipleship between youth and children.

- Have youth visit the church neighborhood just before Christmas and Easter, and share small seasonal gifts they make with the people they meet and invite them to attend upcoming festive worship services. Discuss with the youth their experience of inviting others to come to church and sharing their faith. This discussion and sharing could also be done in front of a local grocery store or mall.

- Develop an e-mail connection between youth and other parishioners, to share stories of faith and inspiration, prayer concerns, and ideas for strengthening the mission and ministry of the church.

Vocation/Ministry

- Have youth participate in a spiritual gifts inventory. Match gifts with various congregational ministries. Invite youth to serve on church council, planning committees, synodical teams. Also encourage youth to serve at church work days, within the education ministry, child care, worship leadership, hospitality team. Nurture young people's gifts by giving them opportunities to serve.

- Use "confirmation stoles" with the young person's name and other symbols of faith embroidered on it. Invite youth to wear the stoles at an Affirmation of Baptism service and at other occasions to reinforce their calling to service through their baptism.

- Have youth host a training session on using computers for ministry and learning for the adults in the congregation.

- Offer a session helping youth to explore ways they can be ministers to their younger siblings and to their parents or guardians, grandparents, and other family members. Create an in-home resource that helps the family understand and practice its role of ministry and service as a family unit. Incorporate family meals that the youth host after regular class sessions. Have youth share what they have learned; conclude with a time of prayer and worship.

- Have a youth and parent class quarterly where they take turns being teachers/students. Have them plan a community service project together. Invite the congregation to participate in the service project.

- Have youth conduct a survey of the local neighborhood regarding what people need and how the church can best serve their needs. Invite youth to share the survey with local governmental agencies and representatives. Explore ways to address these needs through their time and talents.

- Develop a seminar on money and stewardship for youth. Have youth share a program for the congregation on the issue of being a faithful steward of God's gifts. Have youth participate in and then host a welfare simulation game for the congregation.

- Have a career day for youth, inviting various members of the congregation to serve on a panel and share their vocation in light of baptism and service to God. Invite youth to pair up with the member whose career interests them and make arrangements for an on-site visit.

These are only a few examples of how these three themes can help to organize a plan for a comprehensive approach to confirmation ministry. The goal is to integrate confirmation ministry into the overall life of the congregation and inspire a greater sense of ownership by the laity.

Step Four: Working Out the Details

The previous steps all sound fine, except for one thing, working out the details, including questions such as:

- Who is going to do it?

- How long should the program be?

- How should students be grouped together: by age level, by learning abilities, or should learning events be intergenerational?

- What core resources will be needed to implement the program?

- What role will parents play?

- How can meeting times be scheduled that don't conflict with the busy lifestyle of today's families?

These types of practical concerns need to be addressed by the confirmation ministry planning team in light of the mission and program approach that best suits your congregation's ministry. As discussed in chapter 3, congregations need the freedom to experiment with a variety of approaches, including retreats, camping, and cooperative events with other churches, small and large group, individual or in-home study. Whatever approach you select, the important thing is that it meets the needs of the participants, that it is grounded in your overall purpose and mission for confirmation ministry, and that it is evaluated regularly with an openness to try additional new approaches if necessary.

It is important to note that, according to the April 1998 survey, the most effective confirmation programs with youth include the following components:

- The congregation offers a strong youth ministry program in general and often integrates its youth ministry program into its confirmation ministry.

- An intentional learning, service, and fellowship ministry focuses on those who are traditionally considered "post-confirmation" age.

- Strong lay participation and ownership of the confirmation ministry program are encouraged. Although the program relies on a confirmation ministry team to plan it out, congregational experience and expertise serve as partners in confirmation ministry.

- Parental participation includes the sharing of expectations up front with a ministry team that is supportive of the family role.

- The education of the entire congregation emphasizes that confirmation min-

istry is a lifelong process and includes specific programs for children and adult involvement, using customized catechesis programs coupled with repeatable baptismal affirmations.

- A sufficient budget for confirmation ministry is provided, including purchase of resources and funding of training seminars for pastors and lay volunteers to attend.

- Pastors take time to study the purpose of confirmation ministry, attend workshops, and invite congregational members to play an active role in shaping its future program.

In conclusion it is safe to say that confirmation ministry will always be in the process of reformation as we better understand and practice God's purpose for it. A central asset of our Lutheran heritage is the boldness to reform that which needs to be reformed, according to God's Spirit and Word. Confirmation ministry from its conception presents a freedom to explore new ways to strengthen what is working well in your congregation and consider creative alternatives that could enhance the overall mission of faithful baptismal living throughout the church and the world.

The key to the future of confirmation ministry is dialogue and understanding. If this planning guide has given you the opportunity to take a step back from just "doing confirmation" as it has always been done, and allowed you to ask questions and share convictions with regard to why we do confirmation, then the conversation has begun and the hope of promoting dialogue has been accomplished. Of course dialogue requires a number of things to happen. First, dialogue means relationship and relationship means commitment. We must be committed to the gospel and our heritage, and we must also be committed to each other by being honest and attentive. Second, dialogue requires risk. Risk initially sounds frightening, but in the long haul, risk can result in fostering and establishing new confidences and expressions of faith. Third, dialogue means taking advantage of new opportunities that present themselves; new resources, new ideas, new discoveries, all offer new ways of communicating. Finally, dialogue involves a disposition toward change, renewal, and growth. Entering into an honest conversation can inspire the discovery of creative alternatives, individually and communally. Dialogue can give us the ability to understand God's word of truth and the courage to follow its guidance as we embark on the journey of affirming and living our baptismal faith.[2]

Closing Prayer

O gracious Fountain of love and life,
in the waters of baptism
you make us your daughters and sons
    forever.
May our daily affirmation and celebration
    of baptism
be a lamp to our feet and a light to our
    path.
Help us be witnesses to your ongoing work
    and ministry in the church,
begun at baptism
and completed at the final confirmation of
    the resurrection. Amen

Reflection and Discussion Questions

1. What would you like your confirmation ministry to look like in the next five, ten, and twenty years? What will be your guiding principles and mission statement?

2. What specific steps can you take to promote dialogue and constructive conversation within your congregation in helping your members understand and develop the purpose of confirmation ministry?

3. What role do you want to play in helping to shape, guide, and implement your congregation's confirmation ministry?

Notes

1. *The Use of the Means of Grace: A Statement on the Practice of Word and Sacrament*, adopted at the ELCA Churchwide Assembly, August 19, 1997, 25.

2. See Eugene C. Kreider, "Confirmation: Convictions and Practices," *Word and World*, vol. 11, no. 4 (Fall 1991), 394-395. The entire issue is devoted to the subject of confirmation ministry.

Pre-Study Questionnaire

This questionnaire is to be completed before reading the planner.

Name of team member:

_____

Name of congregation:

_____

City/State of congregation:

_____

1. Which of the following statements best describes your definition and theological understanding of confirmation ministry? *(Number statements 1 to 6, with 1 being most accurate and 6 being least accurate.)*

__ Confirmation is an instructional program for adolescent youth in the church, to help prepare them to become adult members.

__ Confirmation is a program to examine and prepare youth to complete and claim the vows that were made at their baptism.

__ Confirmation is a pastoral and educational ministry of the church that helps the baptized through word and sacrament to identify more deeply with the Christian community and participate more fully in its mission.

__ Confirmation is a rite of passage that helps move the adolescent youth into becoming a responsible adult member of the church, familiar with and committed to its tradition and practices.

__ Confirmation is the lifelong process of being shaped by our baptism and the ministry of affirming the power baptism has in strengthening our participation with the Christian community and its mission to the world.

__ Confirmation is the public act of confirming one's faith and making a vow of commitment to Christ.

__ Other: _____

_____

_____

2. Which of the following statements best describe your understanding of the central purpose of confirmation ministry? *(Number statements 1 to 5, with 1 being most accurate and 5 being least accurate.)*

__ To prepare adolescent youth to become adult members of the church.

__ To teach adolescent youth the basic doctrines and traditions of the church.

__ To serve as a pastoral and educational ministry for affirmation of baptism at all ages.

__ To complete and claim the promises made at baptism.

__ To serve as a tool for ongoing faith formation and lifelong learning.

__ Other: _____

_____

_____

3. The process by which the central purpose of confirmation ministry may be accomplished includes several possible approaches. Please indicate which approaches you feel are most essential. *(Prioritize each approach, with 1 being most essential and 7 being least essential, or N/E if you feel it is not essential.)*

__ A program of instruction for a specific and limited amount of time.

__ A public ceremony or rite of confirmation.

__ An ongoing educational ministry that incorporates repeatable affirmations of baptism with various lifelong learning events.

__ A relational-based program that emphasizes community through small group learning activities.

__ A mentor program that includes other church members to serve as guides in learning and ministry.

__ An in-home program that enables parents to be the primary partners in shaping faith.

__ A program that includes experiential learning events and community service projects.

__ Other: _____
_____
_____

4. Who do you think should be responsible for implementing confirmation/affirmation of baptism ministry? *(Number items 1 to 6, with 1 for most responsible and 6 for least responsible.)*

__ the whole congregation

__ the pastor

__ a confirmation ministry team

__ the Christian education committee

__ parents

__ students

__ other: _____
_____
_____

5. What do you see as the most positive aspects to your current confirmation ministry program?

6. What do you see as the most frustrating and least positive aspects within your current confirmation program? How would you change it if you could?

7. What resources do you find most helpful in your confirmation ministry? List specific examples of curriculum if possible.

8. What additional resources do you need or would like to see made available?

Post-Study Questionnaire

This questionnaire is to be completed after reading the planner.

Name of team member:

_____

Name of congregation:

_____

City/State of congregation:

_____

1. After reading and discussing this planner, which definition and theological understanding of confirmation ministry most accurately describes your view? *(Number statements 1 to 6, with 1 being most accurate and 6 being least accurate.)*

___ Confirmation is an instructional program for adolescent youth in the church, to help prepare them to become adult members.

___ Confirmation is a program to examine and prepare youth to complete and claim the vows that were made at their baptism.

___ Confirmation is a pastoral and educational ministry of the church that helps the baptized through word and sacrament to identify more deeply with the Christian community and participate more fully in its mission.

___ Confirmation is a rite of passage that helps move the adolescent youth into becoming a responsible adult member of the church, familiar with and committed to its tradition and practices.

___ Confirmation is the lifelong process of being shaped by our baptism and the ministry of affirming the power baptism has in strengthening our participation with the Christian community and its mission to the world.

___ Confirmation is the public act of confirming one's faith and making a vow of commitment to Christ.

___ Other: _____

_____

_____

Has your view changed? Additional comments:

_____

_____

2. After reading and discussing this planner, what is your understanding of the central purpose of confirmation ministry? *(Number statements 1 to 5, with 1 being most accurate and 5 being least accurate.)*

___ To prepare adolescent youth to become adult members of the church.

___ To teach adolescent youth the basic doctrines and traditions of the church.

___ To serve as a pastoral and educational ministry for affirmation of baptism at all ages.

___ To complete and claim the promises made at baptism.

___ To serve as a tool for ongoing faith formation and lifelong learning.

___ Other: _____

_____

_____

Has your view changed? Additional comments:

_____

_____

3. After reading and discussing this planner, which approach or approaches do you believe are most essential to accomplishing the central purpose of confirmation ministry? Please indicate which approaches you feel are most essential. *(Prioritize each approach, with 1 being most essential and 7 being least essential, or N/E if you feel it is not essential.)*

___ A program of instruction for a specific and limited amount of time.

___ A public ceremony or rite of confirmation.

___ An ongoing educational ministry that incorporates repeatable affirmations of baptism with various lifelong learning events.

___ A relational-based program that emphasizes community through small group learning activities.

___ A mentor program that includes other church members to serve as guides in learning and ministry.

___ An in-home program that enables parents to be the primary partners in shaping faith.

___ A program that includes experiential learning events and community service projects.

___ Other: _____

_____

_____

Has your view changed? Additional comments:

_____

_____

4. After reading and discussing this planner, who do you think should be responsible for implementing confirmation/affirmation of baptism ministry? *(Number items 1 to 6, with 1 for most responsible and 6 for least responsible.)*

___ the whole congregation

___ the pastor

___ a confirmation ministry team

___ the Christian education committee

___ parents

___ students

___ other: _____

_____

_____

Has your view changed? Additional comments:

_____

_____

5. What do you see as the largest hurdle for your congregation in adopting an expanded approach to confirmation ministry that is lifelong and offers repeatable affirmations of baptism? *(Check all items that apply.)*

___ Practical problems of implementing this approach.

___ Resistance to changing/expanding the traditional definition and practice of confirmation.

___ The need to educate the congregation about confirmation ministry.

___ Lack of parental involvement.

___ Lack of congregational involvement.

___ The need for resources/curriculum to implement this approach.

___ The need for pastors to be educated and trained in this approach.

___ Other: _____

_____

_____

6. How can the national synod office, local synod office, and the publishing house best assist you in addressing these concerns? *(Check all items that apply, and prioritize 1 through 5.)*

___ Offer a variety of specific and inexpensive resources and curriculum guides.

___ Train leaders through workshops and seminars at synod assemblies and within congregations.

___ Make sure pastors are being educated in the field of confirmation ministry at seminary and through continuing education events.

___ Develop ways to network leadership and resources.

___ Encourage congregations develop their vision for confirmation ministry and establish confirmation teams to study the issue and make recommendations to the congregation.

___ Other: _____

_____

_____

6. Do you believe that confirmation ministry should be practiced in the same way in all Lutheran congregations or should it be left up to individual congregations to shape a program that fits their needs and context? What elements should remain uniformly practiced? What elements should be flexible? Please explain.

7. After reading and discussing this planner, what do you see as your next step (or steps) toward implementing your vision for confirmation ministry in your congregation?

Confirmation Ministry Team

The following sections describe the guidelines for the establishment of a confirmation ministry team and include space for writing ideas about your own confirmation ministry team.

Structure

The structure of the team should reflect the size and general makeup of the congregation, including such aspects as culture, ethnicity, age, length of membership, and so on. It should also reflect the various ministries of the congregation or congregations. (In some situations, two or more congregations may combine together to create a joint ministry team.) The team may include the pastor, other congregational leaders (such as a council member or worship committee member), educational leaders (from within the congregation and from the wider community), youth, parents, and godparents. The team size may vary according to interest and the number of volunteers.

Our structure:

Purpose

The purpose of the team is to define what confirmation ministry means in the particular context of the congregation. It should work on expanding the ownership of the ministry, guide planning and implementation, and relate confirmation ministry to the congregation's total ministry.

The team will be responsible for regular review and evaluation of the program with regard to the overriding themes of baptismal faith, identity, vocation, and community.

Our purpose:

Format

The team will meet regularly to assess or monitor the vision of confirmation ministry as it relates to the congregation's mission. Team members will review and evaluate new resources and opportunities to strengthen the overall program. This review may include such activities as attending training workshops and curriculum seminars, and networking with other congregations. The team will have as part of its purpose to be supportive of pastoral and lay teachers and be sensitive to student needs.

Our format:

Tasks

Some examples of specific tasks to be done include the following:

- Study the congregation's mission statement and examine how confirmation ministry fits in terms of total mission and ministry.

- Help educate the congregation on the vital role of confirmation ministry and explore ways to integrate existing church programs with confirmation programs and a broader application of baptismal affirmation. Specific focus should include new member classes, youth group activities, pre- and postbaptismal sessions, intergenerational learning events, and other study groups.

- Identify members who are committed to teaching or to curriculum development. Recruit them to assist in finding new resources and implementing the program. Recruit one person to serve as confirmation ministry coordinator.

- Develop financial support for confirmation ministry, including funding for pastoral and lay training events.

- Increase visibility of the confirmation ministry program and invite a broader range of congregational responsibility, such as adult mentors, participation in cooperative and experiential learning events (including taking confirmands to visit other religious houses of worship, a mortuary, or a nursing home), in-home programs, providing meals after a time of instruction, and most importantly, inviting them to become ongoing students in the process of a lifelong learning confirmation program.

- Develop a long-range plan for making confirmation ministry inclusive of the entire church community. Promote biblical literacy and appreciation for Luther's Small Catechism across all age levels.

- Set up specific guidelines to ensure that the confirmation ministry program be gospel-centered and grace-centered both in content and in approach.

- Encourage a spirit of flexibility and creativity coupled with an appreciation for tradition and the Lutheran heritage when exploring new alternatives and resources.

- Promote ecumenical partnerships for the development of mutual baptismal affirmation programs.

Our tasks:

Confirmation Ministry Assessment Tool

Goal: To offer a program that focuses on God's grace through baptismal living as it shapes our understanding and practice of identity/community, mission/discipleship, and vocation/ministry.

QUESTIONS

— How are we reminding people of the dynamic power of baptism as a resource for facing the transitions of life?

— How do we help people to use the disciplines of faith (prayer, study of God's word, service, worship) to make decisions about their lives as baptized people?

— How are we modeling what baptismal living means and looks like?

— Do we know how to share our faith story?

Goal: To offer a program that deepens appreciation and reliance upon the Bible and Luther's Small Catechism as key resources for the baptismal journey.

QUESTIONS

— How are we making use of the classic "question and answer" catechesis approach to learning and seeking for the truth?

— How are we using relevant modes of communication to make the Bible and the Small Catechism accessible?

— Do we offer positive models for lifelong learning through Bible study and catechism for all ages?

Goal: To offer a program developed by the congregation to fit its overall mission statement and in accordance with its vision and guidelines.

QUESTIONS

— Do we have a responsible leadership team that regularly evaluates our confirmation ministry program as it relates to our congregation's ministry as a whole?

— Are the goals and expectations of the program clearly formulated and made known to all involved?

— Does the leadership team include youth and parent members who have a sense of ownership in the development of the program?

— Has our pastoral and lay teaching staff received training and support?

— What happens to the program if the pastor leaves?

— How can laity take a more active role in the responsibility for the confirmation program?

Goal: To offer a program that strengthens relationships within the congregation and the wider community.

QUESTIONS

— How can our program benefit from mentors who serve as mature disciples and examples of faith?

— How can our program involve community service projects that link participants to a ministry to the world?

— How can we encourage training and support for baptismal sponsors?

— Do members remain active after being involved in an affirmation of baptism rite?

— Do we offer retreats, camping experiences, and cooperative learning events with other congregations?

Goal: To integrate the program into our worship, devotional, and prayer life, with an emphasis on the daily affirmation of God's baptismal grace.

QUESTIONS

__ What in-home resources do we provide for individuals and families?

__ Do we encourage parents and siblings in partnered learning experiences?

__ How do we promote faith conversation to take place beyond the church grounds?

__ Are we drawing from the ancient church disciplines and resources to help shape our confirmation program?

__ How are the congregation's education and worship ministries working to support each other?

__ What opportunities are provided to invite confirmands to be actively involved in worship and prayer?

Goal: To develop and promote a program that emphasizes affirmation of baptism as a lifelong process rather than a once-in-a-lifetime event.

QUESTIONS

__ Do we offer repeatable baptismal affirmation rites based upon life transitions and teachable moments?

__ Do we offer a program that draws upon life's baptismal rhythms of dying and raising in organizing opportunities for ministry in the congregation?

__ How can we invite members to see confirmation as a ministry inclusive of the whole church?

__ Does our confirmation program still lead to becoming "adult" members of the church, rather than the lifelong process of being faithful church members?

__ Does our confirmation program offer a safe place for people to honestly examine and explore their faith journeys?

__ How does our confirmation ministry include people who are new to the faith, or those who desire to develop a deeper sense of discipleship and commitment through baptismal affirmation?

__ How are we encouraging our youth to see confirmation as a lifelong process of baptismal affirmation and not a graduation?

(See also *Confirmation Ministry Task Force Report*, 1993, 12-13; and *Confirmation: More Than Just Business as Usual!*, 1998, 11-13.)